Massachusetts

By Sarah De Capua

Consultants
Nanci Vargus, Ed.D.
Primary Multiage Teacher
Decatur Township Schools, Indianapolis, Indiana

Katharine A. Kane, Reading Specialist
Former Language Arts Coordinator
San Diego County Office of Education

Children's Press®
A Division of Scholastic Inc.
New York   Toronto   London   Auckland   Sydney
Mexico City   New Delhi   Hong Kong
Danbury, Connecticut

Designer: Herman Adler Design
Photo Researcher: Caroline Anderson
The photo on the cover shows a beach and lighthouse at Martha's Vineyard
in Massachusetts.

Library of Congress Cataloging-in-Publication Data

De Capua, Sarah.
  Massachusetts / by Sarah De Capua.
      p. cm. — (Rookie read-about geography)
Includes index.
Summary: Introduces the geography, animals, tourist sites, and other
facts about the state in which Pilgrims came ashore in the year 1620.
  ISBN 0-516-22666-5 (lib. bdg.)   0-516-27491-0 (pbk.)
  1. Massachusetts—Juvenile literature. 2. Massachusetts—Geography—
Juvenile literature. [1. Massachusetts.] I. Title. II. Series.
  F64.3 .D36 2002
  974.4—dc21   2002005490

JE
DEC
$14.25
C. 1

1 2 3 4 5 6 7 8 9 10 R 11 10 09 08 07 06 05 04 03 02

Do you know where you
can find Plymouth Rock?

It is in the state of
Massachusetts!

Can you find Massachusetts
on this map? It is located
in the northeast part of
the United States.

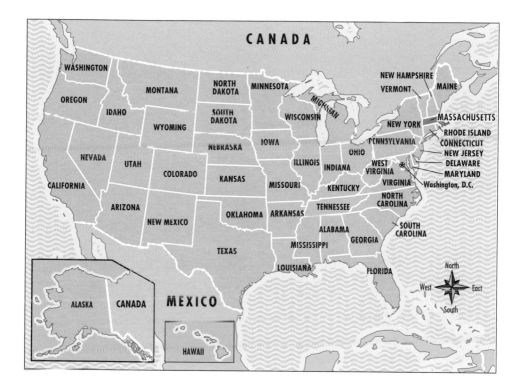

CANADA

WASHINGTON
OREGON
IDAHO
MONTANA
NORTH DAKOTA
MINNESOTA
WYOMING
SOUTH DAKOTA
WISCONSIN
MICHIGAN
NEW HAMPSHIRE
VERMONT
MAINE
NEW YORK
MASSACHUSETTS
RHODE ISLAND
CONNECTICUT
NEW JERSEY
DELAWARE
MARYLAND
Washington, D.C.
NEVADA
UTAH
NEBRASKA
IOWA
ILLINOIS
INDIANA
OHIO
PENNSYLVANIA
WEST VIRGINIA
VIRGINIA
CALIFORNIA
COLORADO
KANSAS
MISSOURI
KENTUCKY
NORTH CAROLINA
ARIZONA
NEW MEXICO
OKLAHOMA
ARKANSAS
TENNESSEE
SOUTH CAROLINA
TEXAS
MISSISSIPPI
ALABAMA
GEORGIA
LOUISIANA
FLORIDA

ALASKA
CANADA
MEXICO

HAWAII

North
West East
South

5

Many different kinds of land can be found in Massachusetts. There are mountains, sand dunes, beaches, and bogs.

7

8

The mountains are called the Berkshire Hills. They are located in the western part of Massachusetts. Mount Greylock is found there. It is the highest place in Massachusetts.

The part of Massachusetts that looks like a curved arm is called Cape Cod. It is famous for its beautiful sand dunes and beaches.

Cape Cod is a peninsula (puh-NIN-suh-luh). It is connected to Massachusetts on one side. The other three sides stick out into the Atlantic Ocean.

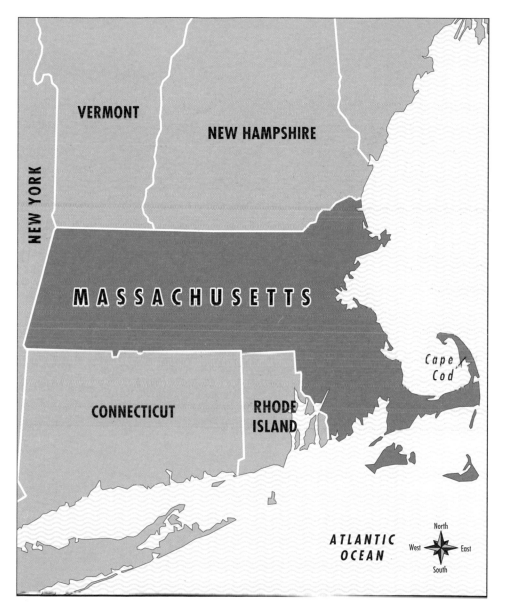

VERMONT

NEW HAMPSHIRE

NEW YORK

MASSACHUSETTS

Cape Cod

CONNECTICUT

RHODE ISLAND

ATLANTIC OCEAN

North
West · East
South

11

Rocky beaches are
found along the
Massachusetts coast.

Fishing is an important job on the coast. Scallops, cod, and flounder caught here are shipped all over the United States.

Boston

Boston is the largest city in Massachusetts. It is also the state capital. It is located on the coast of Massachusetts. Other large cities in Massachusetts include Springfield and Worcester.

Many people in the cities work in banks, computer companies, and other businesses. Other people work in factories and make shoes, cloth, paper, and machines.

Massachusetts also has small towns, such as Lunenburg and Webster. Many people who live near small towns farm for a living. Farmers grow vegetables and raise cattle.

The best farmland in Massachusetts is located in the western half of the state next to the Connecticut River.

Along the coast, cranberries are grown in bogs. Bogs are areas of wet land that hold water like a sponge.

Animals such as deer, beavers, foxes, and many kinds of birds live all over Massachusetts. The state bird is the chickadee.

Massachusetts has snowy winters and warm summers. During the warm summers, many people go to the beaches on the islands of Nantucket and Martha's Vineyard. An island is a piece of land with water all around it.

Where is your favorite
place in Massachusetts?

Words You Know

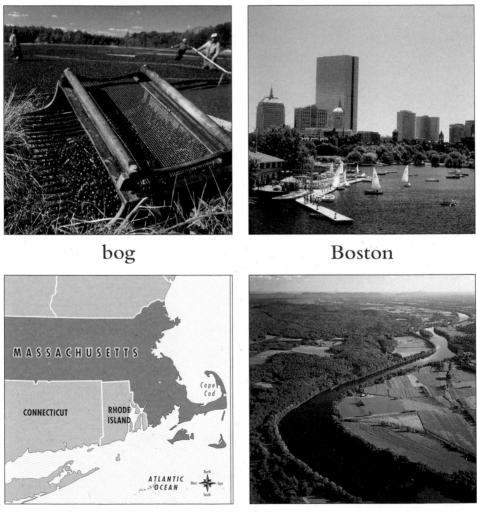

bog

Boston

Cape Cod

farmland

fishing

Mount Greylock

Plymouth Rock

sand dunes

31

Index

About the Author

Sarah De Capua is an author and editor of children's books. She resides in Colorado.

Photo Credits

Photographs © 2002: International Stock Photo/Steve Myers: cover; Kindra Clineff: 7 bottom left, 14, 22, 30 top right, 30 top left; Landslides Aerial Photography/Alex S. MacLean: 21, 30 bottom right; Nance S. Trueworthy: 7 top right, 7 bottom right, 31 bottom right; Stock Boston: 8, 31 top right (C.J. Allen), 12 (Michael Dwyer), 7 top left, 25 (William Johnson), 17 (Shopper), 18 (Frank Siteman), 29 (Brian Smith), 13, 31 top left (Susan Van Etten), 26 (David Weintraub), 3, 31 bottom left (Cary Wolinsky).

Maps by Bob Italiano